LABRADOR RETRIEVERS

MARYSA STORM

BLACK RABBIT BOOKS

Bolt Jr. is published by Black Rabbit Books
P.O. Box 3263, Mankato, Minnesota, 56002.
www.blackrabbitbooks.com

Catherine Cates, designer; Omay Ayres, photo researcher

Names: Storm, Marysa, author.
Title: Labrador retrievers / by Marysa Storm.
Description: Mankato, Minnesota : Black Rabbit Books, [2021] | Series: Bolt Jr. our favorite dogs | Includes bibliographical references and index. | Audience: Ages 6-8 | Audience: Grades K-1 | Summary: "Teaches readers all about Labrador retrievers through simple text, infographics, and fun facts"– Provided by publisher.
Identifiers: LCCN 2019026817 (print) | LCCN 2019026818 (ebook) | ISBN 9781623104702 (hardcover) | ISBN 9781644664568 (paperback) | ISBN 9781623105006 (ebook)
Subjects: LCSH: Labrador retriever–Juvenile literature.
Classification: LCC SF429.L3 S77 2021 (print) | LCC SF429.L3 (ebook) | DDC 636.752/7–dc23
LC record available at https://lccn.loc.gov/2019026817
LC ebook record available at https://lccn.loc.gov/2019026818

Image Credits

AP Images: Patrick Record, 12; iStock: Eriklam, Cover; Shutterstock: Ase, Cover; Ekaterina Brusnika, 20–21; Eric Isselee, 4, 6–7; foxhound photos, 22–23; Grigorita Ko, 18–19; Leoniek van der Vliet, 21; loveaum, 6–7; Master1305, 10; Naddya, 3, 24; Nigel Kirby Photography, 5; Paul Clifton, 6–7; Petrovic Igor, 14; SikorskiFotografie, 8–9; stocksre, 16–17; Susan Schmitz, 1; Tina Rencelj, 10–11; Tosha174, 13

Contents

CHAPTER 1

Meet the Labrador Retriever

The Labrador **retriever** looks up at its owner. The dog's tail wags. Back and forth. Back and forth. The happy dog is waiting for its human to throw the ball. When the boy does, the Lab races off.

retriever: a dog that has a water-resistant coat and is used to find and bring back game

COMPARING HEIGHTS

Labradror retriever

21.5 to 24.5 inches

(55 to 62 centimeters)

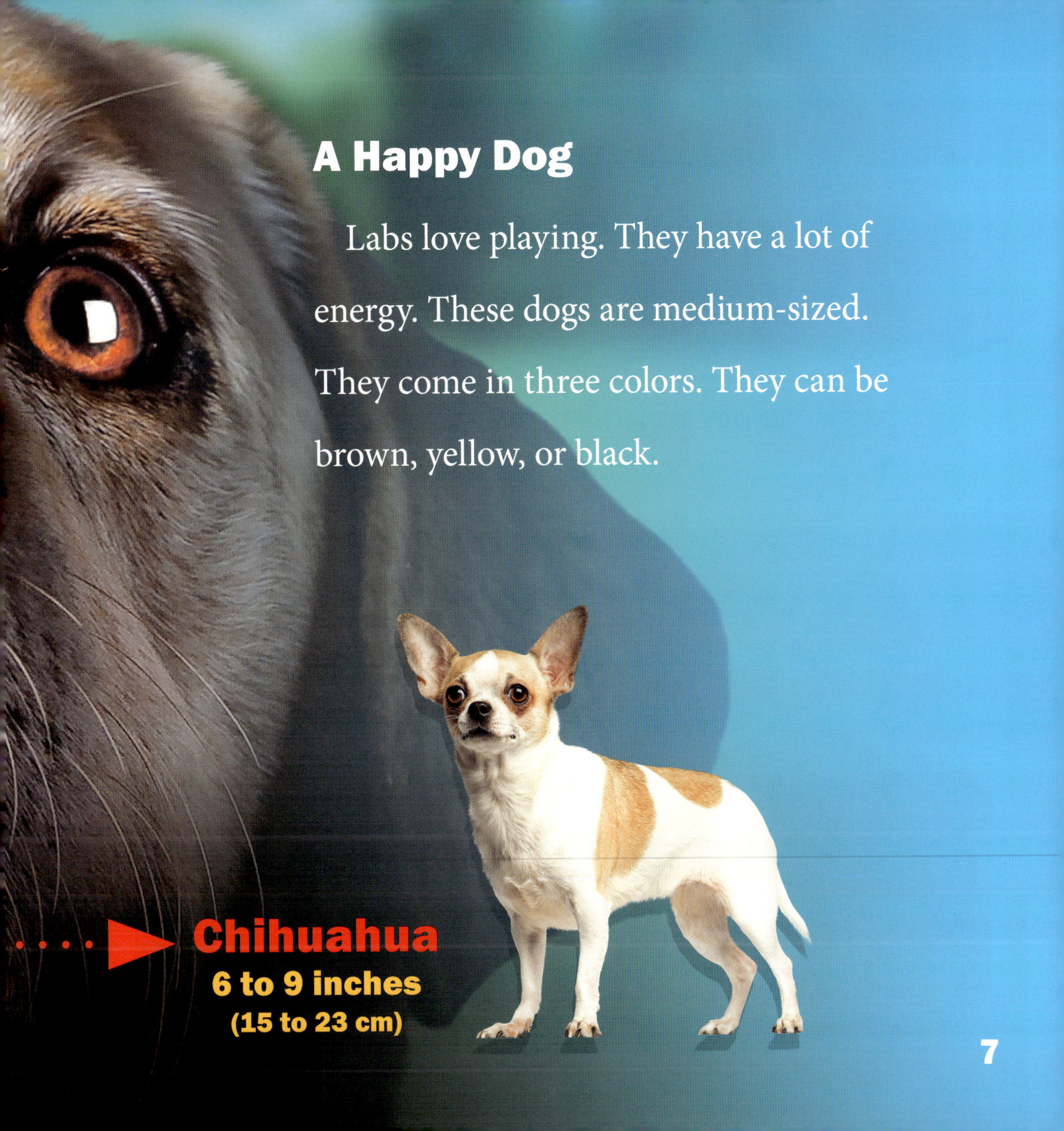

A Happy Dog

Labs love playing. They have a lot of energy. These dogs are medium-sized. They come in three colors. They can be brown, yellow, or black.

Chihuahua
6 to 9 inches
(15 to 23 cm)

PARTS OF A Labrador Retriever

nose
paws

CHAPTER 2

Puppy Personality

Labs are **kind** dogs. They enjoy playing. Labs love helping their owners too. Most need jobs, like getting the paper, to be happy.

kind: wanting or liking to do good

FACT

Labs are great swimmers.

Training

Labs are easy to train. They like following **commands**. Some are trained to help **disabled** people. These dogs can turn on lights. They open doors.

command: an order given to do something

disabled: unable to do normal activities because of an illness or other problem

Where Labrador Retrievers Came From

CHAPTER 3

Labrador Retriever Care

These dogs are easy to care for. They don't need much grooming. But they do need lots of exercise. They need to be around people too.

FACT
Labs' teeth need brushing.

Friends for Life

Labs are friendly dogs. They make great pets for many families. Labs have a lot of energy. But owners say that's part of the joy.

Labrador Retrievers' Weight

55 to 80 pounds (25 to 36 kilograms)

Bonus Facts

Puppies weigh about 1 pound (.5 kg).

Labs live 10 to 12 years.

Brown labs are called chocolate.

Labs have webbed paws.

webbed: having skin between the fingers or toes

READ MORE/WEBSITES

Frank, Sarah. *Labrador Retrievers.* Who's a Good Dog? Minneapolis: Lerner Publications, 2019.

Rustad, Martha E. H. *Labrador Retrievers.* Favorite Dog Breeds. Mankato, MN: Amicus High Interest/Amicus Ink, 2018.

Sternberg, Julie. *Puppy, Puppy, Puppy.* Honesdale, PA: Boyds Mills Press, an imprint of Highlights, 2017.

Labrador Retriever
a-z-animals.com/animals/labrador-retriever/

Labrador Retriever Dog Breed Information
www.akc.org/dog-breeds/labrador-retriever/

The Labrador Retriever – Dogs 101
www.animalplanet.com/tv-shows/dogs-101/videos/the-labrador-retriever

GLOSSARY

command (kuh-MAND)—an order given to do something

disabled (dys-A-buhld)—unable to do normal activities because of an illness or other problem

kind (KAHYND)—wanting or liking to do good

retriever (re-TREE-ver)—a dog that has a water-resistant coat and is used to find and bring back game

webbed (WEBD)—having skin between the fingers or toes

INDEX